I was blessed to hear P.   he
had a profound impact o   at
have lasted until today. I   )k
which is certainly "RE-awakening" me to the Divine in new
ways and voices. As always, Paul makes lively connections
between the spiritual traditions and poetic inspirations of
East and West. I highly recommend that you pray with this
book and savor it!

BROTHER MICKEY MCGRATH, OSFS, *author of Madonnas of Color*

Paul Coutinho has done it again! He has crafted a fine and
practical work of intrafaith engagement, one that engages
where we are in our faith journey with the wider community of fellow sojourners. These contemplative reflections will
truly transform your spirit. Enter the Mystery as you walk
through these fifty-two mini spiritual exercises.

BRYAN FROEHLE, *author of The Disappearing God Gap?*

In his new book, Paul Coutinho offers pebbles of inspiration
for divine awakenings. But in our polarized and fragmented
age, many of these reflections land more like "boulders" of
sanity, calm, and clarity. In the tradition of a spiritual master,
his pithy reflections begin with carefully selected passages
from the world's sacred readings around which he provides
a feast of images, metaphors, and practical spiritual insights.
His book is a testimony to the truth of a quote from Swami
Vivekananda in the first reflection: "You have to grow from
the inside out."

MARK MARKULY, *Dean Emeritus: School of Theology
and Ministry Seattle University*

In Paul Coutinho's beautiful new book we are privileged to experience the meeting between Eastern spiritualities and Ignatian spirituality. The result is an encounter with lasting calm and deep peace, an invitation to meet God in a gentle way. Paul Coutinho's books always invite readers to see life with both open eyes and eyes of faith."

JAMES MARTIN, SJ, *author of Learning to Pray*

Awaken to the Divine by Paul Coutinho offers fifty-two reflections that will nourish your spirit and invite you to deepen your own contemplative prayer practice. Coutinho outlines a way to approach and use the book in order to deepen one's own sense of God consciousness. Integrating the Benedictine prayer form of "Lectio Divina" with the Ignatian prayer of repose found in the Spiritual Exercises with the Hindu stage of wisdom consciousness "Nididhyasana," Coutinho invites the reader to rediscover their own Divine identity, to open up to wisdom, and love and to live a life of embodied wisdom. Spiritual directors and those seeking to deepen their own prayer life will find this book a contemplative treasure trove to be slowly savored!

VALERIE LESNIAK, *Emerita Professor of Spirituality, Seattle University*

PAUL COUTINHO

Awaken
TO THE
Divine

52
CONTEMPLATIVE
REFLECTIONS
TO TRANSFORM
YOUR SPIRIT

**TWENTY-THIRD
PUBLICATIONS**
twentythirdpublications.com

Twenty-Third Publications
977 Hartford Turnpike Unit A
Waterford, CT 06385
(860) 437-3012 or (800) 321-0411
www.twentythirdpublications.com

Cover photo: © stock.adobe.com/Stillfx

ISBN: 978-1-62785-745-1
Printed in the U.S.A.

 A division of Bayard, Inc.

CONTENTS

PART II

Opening Up to Wisdom and Love

PART III

Living with Purpose, Peace, and Joy

INTRODUCTION

The only graces and gifts we possess
are those we have allowed ourselves
to receive and share with others.
I cast pebbles of inspiration, and as the ripples begin,
I consciously detach myself from the fruits of my ministry.

The gifts we have given away become the platform for receiving better and deeper graces. This has been my motivation for all my ministries: teaching, retreats, spiritual direction—and yes, in writing all my books.

In all my ministries I realize that I am just a channel. My constant prayer is this: "Cleanse my heart and my lips that I may worthily proclaim You." I spend time trying to get my ego out of the way, so that the Spirit might work effectively in the minds and hearts of people.

Every now and then I receive confirmation that I am on the right path:

- A woman who attended one of my retreats more than twenty-five years ago told me that that experience continues to sustain her in her daily life. She has made a mantra that I shared her very own: I am Important, Precious, Beautiful!

- Couples on their silver wedding anniversary remind me of the message I shared on their wedding day.
- In my course evaluations, students state how my course was life-changing. I hear how my books have changed people's lives.
- And sometimes, I hear people tell me that they finally get what I have been trying to say for ten years.

This is the Spirit confirming that I am on the right track, and it is encouragement to continue. For my part, while taking in this affirmation, I look for ways to be a better channel, to get my ego out of the way. In accepting the Spirit's confirmation, I take comfort in Mary's Magnificat prayer:

> My soul magnifies the Lord,
>   and my spirit rejoices in God my Savior,
> for he has looked with favor on the lowliness
>   of his servant.
>   Surely, from now on all generations
>   will call me blessed;
> for the Mighty One has done great things for me,
>   and holy is his name. + LUKE 1:46-49

I would like to propose a methodology for the spiritual life and reading of this book. I invite you, dear reader, to open your mind and soul to these three stages:

UNDERSTAND — BELIEVE — KNOW

Many of the inspirational quotes I've chosen for reflection are easy to *understand*. We can grow to *believe* some of these quotes. But there are very few that we *know*. The Eastern understanding of "knowing" or knowledge is that which touches the heart and transforms life. The biblical definition of knowledge goes even deeper. It is *intimacy at the core of our being*.

We will undertake this method through the insights of Sts. Benedict and Ignatius and through perspectives drawn from the Eastern tradition.

St. Benedict's gift for us

Lectio Divina, a form of prayer encouraged by St. Benedict, has four steps. We begin with *Lectio*, Latin for **reading**. The reading could be a passage from the Scriptures or any inspirational literature. The second step is *Meditatio*, **reflection**. This is a reflection on the passage (the *Lectio*). We spend time thinking about a word, a phrase, or an idea that draws our minds and hearts. This is followed by *Oratio*, **response**. This takes the form of a prayer. The final stage is *Contemplatio*, **repose**. In this resting contemplative state, we allow the Divine Presence to take deeper root at the core of our being.

St. Ignatius' gift for us

In the Spiritual Exercises, St. Ignatius introduces us to three major levels of prayer. Meditation, which is the prayer of the mind; Contemplation, which is the prayer of the heart; and the Application of the Senses, which is the prayer of consciousness. In Meditation, one gets revelations and ends the prayer by making resolutions. In Contemplation, one opens oneself to the mystery that is the subject of one's prayer. This allows one to be filled by, transformed by, and drawn into that mystery. The Application of Senses is the prayer where neither the head nor the heart gets in the way of pure consciousness. It is a prayer of spiritual repose.

Spiritual repose is a state of being, when pure consciousness becomes a way of life. We now learn to live as the I–Now–Here. The I is the image and likeness of God, or the Divine Breath. This present moment, NOW, is part of every moment from the beginning to the end of time. Therefore, this NOW is part of eternal time. This place, HERE, where I am now present, is a part of everywhere. It is part of the whole of Creation. In this I–NOW–HERE state, we experience spiritual repose. Spiritual repose gives us the energy and the inspiration to live every moment as if it were our first, our last, and the only moment. We live life as fully human and fully alive! We live the life that Jesus came to give us: Life in all its fullness (John 10:10).

We become contemplative in action. That is, *we open ourselves to the mystery of the Divine Presence at every moment in the here and now* and allow ourselves to be filled and transformed into the mystery of the Divine Essence. We are fully involved in life, with our hearts rooted and grounded in the Divine Essence.

Eastern spirituality's gift for us

The goal of Eastern spirituality is the realization that every part of Creation is Divine. We attain liberation and freedom in this lifetime. I would like to reflect on an ancient Hindu Scripture, the *Upanishad*. One of the meanings of the word *Upanishad* is to sit at the feet of an enlightened teacher. These teachers offer their wisdom to any sincere seeker, through a threefold process: *Sravana, Manana, Nididhyasana.*

Sravana literally means **listening**. In this stage, we begin by listening to the teachings of the sages.

Manana is a stage where we **reflect deeply** on the teachings we have listened to. We spend time trying to understand the teaching through study and reflection.

Nididhyasana is the culmination of *Sravana* and *Manana*. This is the stage when **knowledge becomes wisdom**. This wisdom emanates from us spontaneously, from the core of our being, and its effects are felt by everyone and everything that comes into our presence. *Nididhyasana* becomes as natural as our breathing.

Try this warm-up exercise as you approach the book's reflections:

1. Notice a sentence or even a word that draws your attention. This is the first step of listening.
2. Now read the rest of the chapter, meditating on that word or sentence or do all you can to understand that word or sentence.
3. Then keep repeating it until it sinks to the core of your being or your unconscious and becomes an integral part of your being.

Let's take an example from the Scriptures that tells me who I am. The Bible tells me that I am the image and likeness of God (Genesis 1) or the Divine Breath (Genesis 2) or a child of God. The Hindu Scriptures define us as *Aham Brahmasmi*: I am Brahman or *Tat Tvam Asi*, you are *THAT*— and *THAT* is the Divine Essence. The Qur'an tells us that God is closer to us than our jugular vein! Pick one of these dictums, repeat it continuously, and listen to how it sounds.

Now try to understand the depth of that truth. Then keep repeating it until it becomes part of every fabric of your being. Once we realize this stage, we may not be aware of how we have changed, but everyone else will. *We emote peace and inner freedom wherever we are.*

The three-stage integration, *understand—believe—know*, is reflected in the parable of the Sower and the Seed (Luke 8:4–15). The seeds that fall by the wayside are like those who **understand** that they are made in the image and likeness of God or the Divine Breath but do not want to go deeper. Some may move on to the next stage and want to **believe** this truth. But these are like seeds that fall on rocky ground, the rational type, who do not allow the truth to take root, or seeds that fall among the thorns, the emotional type, who choke the seed and stunt its growth. And then there are those who are open and prepared to receive the truth. When this truth begins to take root and bear fruit, then they truly **know** the truth. And this truth will make them free.

And now, dear reader, I get out of the way.
In Divine Providence, may the pebbles cast in these pages
ripple to the Spirit's beckoning and to your receptivity
to understand, believe, and know.

PART I

Rediscovering Your Divine Identity

1. If You Meet the Buddha on the Road

You have to grow from the inside out.
None can teach you; none can make you spiritual.
There is no other teacher but your own soul.

SWAMI VIVEKANANDA

The spiritual path is an ongoing journey that culminates in self-knowledge and God-realization. Spiritual growth is a process that goes beyond the physical body and mind, realizing our identity as the soul or Spirit. This Spirit is present in every part of creation. The mystics believe that the soul is part of God; it is the Divine Essence.

In the gospels, we find that Jesus is constantly inviting his followers to "the other shore" and then asking them to launch into the deep. This invitation is to find ourselves deeper and deeper in the Ocean of Divine Love and Infinite Life. The Ocean is not something "out there"; it exists at our core. As we journey deeper, we realize that we are the Ocean. The "other shore" in Buddhism is known as *paramita* or the pinnacle of the spiritual life. It is a state of enlightenment that every spiritual person yearns for. It is an invitation to cross the river of life and get to the other shore. Here we experience oneness with the whole of creation.

Karl Rahner, a great Catholic theologian, once said that the Christian of the future would either be a mystic or cease to exist. What Rahner said about Christians is true of every person and culture in today's world. Consciously or unconsciously, we are all striving to be mystics. We know that a mystic cannot belong to or be contained by any religion. Religion is a raft that takes us to the Ocean of Divine Love and Infinite Life. The question is, once we realize that *we* are this Ocean, do we still need the raft?

It is said that the famous ninth-century Chinese Buddhist monk Lin Chi exhorted his disciples, "If you meet the Buddha on the road, kill him." The road is a metaphor for our spiritual journey, and the Buddha represents all teachers and teachings. Truth is the awareness that the Divine Essence is in every part of creation. The Buddha is like the finger pointing to the moon. Once we have become aware of the moon, we do not depend on teachers, and we do not need any teaching. Enlightenment is realized within us.

The prophet Elijah did not find God in the great wind or the earthquake or the fire but in the sound of sheer silence (1 Kings 19:11–12). For Mahatma Gandhi, Truth was God. He explained Truth as realizing our identity in the Divine Essence and experiencing the interconnectedness of all of life. The source of Truth was his inner voice. "I shall lose my usefulness the moment I stifle the still small voice within," he said (December 3, 1925).

Personal experience was paramount for Ignatius of Loyola, founder of the Jesuits. He was convinced that "when the eyes of his understanding were opened," that is, when he experienced awareness and consciousness of the Essence of life, he did not need the holy Scriptures anymore, nor would he need any external authority.

The prophet Jeremiah invites us to live by a Divine inner and personal covenant:

> This is the covenant that I will make with the house of Israel after those days, says the LORD: I will put my law within them, and I will write it on their hearts; and I will be their God, and they shall be my people. No longer shall they teach one another, or say to each other, "Know the Lord," for they shall all know me, from the least of them to the greatest, says the Lord. + JEREMIAH 31:33-34

Religion, the saints, spiritual teachers, and even the Scriptures are all fingers pointing beyond themselves. They all reveal to us the "other shore."

2. Formless, Nameless Essence

Behind all names and forms is the one nameless,
formless Essence. Behind all sounds, there is
the soundless Supreme Silence.

SRI AUROBINDO

The Infinite is vast, empty, and essentially without form. The Divine is formless and nameless. Naming something gives you power over what you name, assigns a particular character to it, and reflects your relationship with that which you have named. But as soon as you name anything you begin to cut back its essence. When we name God, we diminish God. In the beginning, names are like fingers that point beyond themselves. As time goes on, we seem to get lost in the finger and lose sight of what it points to.

Hinduism has 330 million names for god; 330 million ways of minimizing the Divine Essence. But the 330 million gods are only an expression of experiences of that which is beyond; 330 million disposable images of God until one experiences God as *"TAT"* or *THAT*—God beyond all names—just Being or Essence! Buddhists experience this Essence in the breath, which is part of the Universal and Eternal Energy. This breath is formless and nameless; it just IS. Islam forbids the creation of images of any sentient being and most especially any image of God or the Prophet Muhammad. In the Old Testament, God is YHWH, a name that cannot be pronounced—a God who was revealed as "I AM *THAT* I AM" (Exodus 3:14–15).

Every religious tradition believes that God is Infinite and therefore impossible to conceptualize. We come up with metaphors to explain God to little children and the uneducated. These metaphors are fingers pointing to a reality that is beyond the metaphor. But too often we take the metaphor literally and never experience the Divine Essence. Thomas Aquinas, who had the greatest influence on Christian philosophy and theology, concluded that God is known by what God is not. This is very close to *Neti Neti*, "Not this. Not that"—one of the Indian understandings of God.

Adam and Eve had a momentary glimpse into Essence in the Garden of Eden when they ate the forbidden fruit of knowledge and consciousness. Their eyes were opened and they realized that they were naked. They were enlightened and were able to experience their own Essence in the Ultimate Essence: *THAT*! The Lord God then proceeded to put on skins to cover *THAT*. These skins now become our reality: we define ourselves by our gender, culture, religion. We continue to put skins on everything by naming people, places, things, animals, birds, plants, and other parts of creation. If we learn to look beyond the skins, beyond names, we will begin to experience the Essence once again as the FORMLESS *THAT*! We will begin to live in the realm of the Spirit.

Jesus proclaimed *THAT* as Spirit and Truth and not something that is worshiped on any holy mountain or in any temple (John 4). He invited us to experience *THAT* in the birds of the air and the lilies of the field until we experience all of life in *THAT*. St. Paul exclaims, in *THAT* there is neither Jew nor Gentile, slave or free, male and female (Galatians 3:28)! He explains that through the process of *kenosis*, Jesus shed the skins put on by the Lord God in the Garden of Eden and realized *THAT*. *Kenosis* is the process of emptying ourselves of all our defense mechanisms and celebrating our true divine selves.

3. Beliefs Are Not Always Facts

The unexamined life is not worth living.
SOCRATES

Socrates' insightful and challenging statement prompts us to reexamine whether our beliefs are factual. We were given messages as little children that affect our self-worth. We have had life experiences that have determined our self-image. Social and religious norms have created divisions and hierarchies among people of different nations and cultures. Media images, labels, and propaganda instill fear, hatred, and prejudice against groups of people.

Culture, values, and beliefs are pillars for harmonious living in a community. In every culture, we see how the superiority of a race, caste, and gender evolve. These establish themselves as the dominant part of society. However, community living is dynamic and always evolving. If these pillars do not change with the signs of the times, they will become counterproductive. Unexamined cultural beliefs, traditions, and superstitions have destroyed generations of individuals and groups.

When Karl Marx exclaimed that religion is the opium of the people, he was not condemning religion, but the way religious beliefs are used to disillusion and manipulate people and to sustain the rich and subdue the poor. Marx's statement is critical of the lifestyle and indomitable security of the religious powers. It condemns wars that are initiated and fought in the name of religion. In the face of ignorance and injustice, religion offers a bandage response and renders smart brains dead.

The fruit of the tree of knowledge and consciousness in the Garden of Eden is still forbidden to humans with threats of punishment, alienation, and suffering. Our Divine Essence and oneness are covered with external skins that separate us by race, color, religion, and in myriad other ways. The tree of life is now guarded by religion and culture with flaming swords swinging in every direction.

To test our beliefs against facts, we need to constantly eat the forbidden fruit of knowledge and consciousness. St. Paul gives us an example: when he dared to eat the forbidden fruit, his life was transformed. Paul's belief in the Mosaic Law was absolute, leading to his determination to persecute anyone who broke this sacred law. In particular, he targeted the disciples of Jesus, who were called followers of The Way. When his staunch beliefs were tested against the *facts* of The Way, Paul experienced *metanoia*, a change of heart. The Law of the Spirit now superseded the Mosaic Law. His new beliefs went beyond, and sometimes contradicted, the teachings and practices of the Apostles. Remember, life is dynamic and always evolving, and beliefs must be constantly challenged with new knowledge and facts.

The unexamined life can easily turn into opium that deadens the intellect and the will to respond to human atrocities happening all around us. Have our beliefs evolved with the signs of the times? Do we need a *metanoia* so we can respond to the needs of the world?

4. The Last Dance on the Titanic

*Very truly, I tell you, unless a grain of wheat falls
into the earth and dies, it remains just a single grain;
but if it dies it bears much fruit.*

JOHN 12:24

It is said that we need to have our roots in traditional religion. If these roots are healthy and alive, they will sprout into a beautiful spiritual tree that will welcome creatures of all kinds without any discrimination and offer itself as a home, providing shade and fruit. Ultimately, the tree catapults into the mystical when, in the words of Nobel Laureate Rabindranath Tagore, "The woodcutter's axe begged for its handle from the tree. The tree gave it."

This wise saying of Tagore is often understood to mean that when we give into the needs of others, we may endanger our own. But there is a mystical slant to this. The tree has to allow itself to die in order to live in many different ways. Wood is used in building ships that will connect people and continents; homes that will provide warmth and comfort for families; musical instruments that will awaken the human spirit to the spiritual and mystical; children's toys that bring so much joy.

Our reflection continues with Rabi'a al-Basri, born around 717 CE and considered the first Sufi saint. After her father died, she was captured and sold as a sex slave at the age of eleven. She was forced to sing and dance and otherwise "entertain" people for twenty-five years. One day she had an awakening, and the only songs that would come out of her were songs of her beloved God. Rabi'a believed that everything that happened in her life is according to the Divine plan. She accepted everything as a gift from God, even her life as a sex slave. Nothing could separate her from the bond she had with the Divine. She soon became the mother of many a Sufi mystic and an inspiration for generations to come. She often prayed, "If You had not set me apart by affliction, I would not have increased Your lovers."

In the Spiritual Exercises, St. Ignatius ends his prayer of total offering with the words, "Give me only your love and your grace for this is sufficient for me" (#234). This sentiment is echoed in Rabi'a's famous prayer:

O God, if I worship You for fear of Hell,
Burn me in Hell;
And if I worship You in the hope of Paradise,
Exclude me from Paradise.
But if I worship You for Your Own sake,
Grudge me not Your everlasting Beauty.

St. Ignatius also believed that spiritual pride was the greatest hindrance in our intimacy with God. Rabi'a reflects the same belief in the following encounter. A man who was known to be very religious once boasted that ever since he set upon the path of religion, he had not sinned against God who created him. Rabi'a responded, "Alas my son, your existence is a sin where no other sin may be compared."

Those who are spiritual strive to reach heaven through many spiritual endeavors. These sometimes proclaim, "Religion is for those who do not want to go to hell; spirituality is for those who have been there."

But then there is the mystic for whom heaven and hell are a waste of time. They wake up to the mystery and magic of Creation; they breathe the Divine Breath that permeates all life and creation. They bask in the "I AM THAT I AM" and radiate God who is Spirit and Truth and is not worshiped on any Sacred Mountain or Holy Temple. "Remain in Me, and I in you" becomes their way of life.

With Rabi'a, these mystics' heart-song is this:

> Give the reward of this world to your enemies;
> Give the reward of the next world to your friends.
> You are enough for me.

5. To Live Is to Constantly Seek New Horizons

You can't cross the sea merely by standing and staring at the water.
RABINDRANATH TAGORE

"The mass of men live lives of quiet desperation." This famous quote of Henry David Thoreau was meant to motivate people to follow their passion and live the fullness of life. Thoreau, the transcendentalist, believed that if we follow our dreams and dare to live the lives we imagined, we will cross the sea and find ourselves in the Ocean of Eternal Bliss.

Most people who busy themselves with meaningless activity will not get out of their desperate lives. When material wealth, the pleasures of life, prestige and power become the goal of one's life, they create a vast existential vacuum. Yes, they will get what they want, but it will never be enough. They seem to be always running after something, but they are really just running in place, stuck on a treadmill of desire. We often have great desires but until those desires become an expectation, they are an excuse for doing little or nothing. No one becomes wise simply by reading books, listening to lectures, or following a cult. Neither does a person get drunk by reading the labels on a bottle of alcohol.

Wisdom comes from having an experience that becomes one's truth. The ultimate experience is to encounter the existential question when we find our identity in the Divine and experience an interconnectedness with all of creation.

Ships are safe in the harbor, but that's not what ships were made for. Similarly, many of us merely exist in the security of our little worlds. We begin to live when we venture into the deeper waters of life, when we go beyond the sacred boundaries of our family, country, culture, and religion. Every boundary we cross opens to a new horizon. To live is to constantly seek new horizons. While this journey is travelled outwardly, it is truly experienced by going deeper and deeper into ourselves.

The story of Abraham in the Bible is a classic example of the spiritual journey.

> Now the LORD said to Abram, "Go from your country and your kindred and your father's house to the land that I will show you. I will make of you a great nation, and I will bless you, and make your name great, so that you will be a blessing. I will bless those

who bless you, and the one who curses you I will curse; and in you all the families of the earth shall be blessed." + GENESIS 12:1-3

The human spirit has this relentless quest to realize our full potential and know the limitlessness of our being. If we follow the example of Abraham, we will find the land flowing with milk and honey at the core of our being; we will become one with the stars and the sand on the seashore (Exodus 3:8; Genesis 22:17). We will become Universal.

We must give up our daily routines that numb our minds and kill our inner spirits. We must not settle for the futility and meaninglessness of monotonous life. When we get out of our comfort zones and safety structures provided by our own society, religion, and culture, we regain the wonder and freedom we had when we were little children. Everything becomes mystical and magical once more. We are then truly born again!

6. Forbidden Thought

A forbidden writing is thought to be a certain spark of truth, that flies up in the face of them who seek to tread it out.

FRANCIS BACON

To question is to be alive. Otherwise, we merely exist. Most of us have experiences in our past that we have suppressed, skeletons in our closets that we guard with our lives. We also have teachings, customs, rituals, and practices that have been passed down to us with an implicit or even explicit command that we should not question. This is reflected by Carl Jung's experience of the "forbidden thought."

When Jung was about twelve years old, he had what might be called his foundational experience. He walked by the Cathedral of Basel on his way to school. One day he looked up and saw a beautiful sky and God sitting on his throne, looking down on the cathedral. Like a bolt from out of the blue, he was plagued by a forbidden thought.

He was convinced that if he succumbed to this thought, he would be punished and something terrible would happen to him. He could not talk to his father or his nine uncles who were part of the clergy in the Swiss Reform Church, since every time Jung asked a question, he was told that it was in the Bible and that was the end of the conversation. He was tormented by the forbidden thought and knew he would have to deal with it by himself.

On the third day, he began to think that this challenge came from the all-powerful and all-knowing God. Giving in to this temptation would go against the teachings of religion and against God's own commandment! But the intensity of the forbidden thought overpowered him. Jung turned his gaze to God sitting on his golden throne, high above the world, and from under the throne, an enormous turd fell upon the sparkling new roof of the cathedral, shattering it and breaking the solid walls. At that moment he experienced unutterable bliss, such as he had never known, and spiritual freedom that would be the foundation of the rest of his life.

Following this experience, Jung deliberated long about what God's will might be and why on earth he would attack his own cathedral.

The forbidden thought is like the forbidden fruit in the Garden of Eden. "You shall not eat of the fruit of the tree that is in the middle of the garden, nor shall you touch it, or you shall die" (Genesis 3:3). Not only did Adam and Eve touch the fruit, but they also ate it. They experienced enlightenment when their eyes were opened and they realized their nakedness. They became conscious of their true essence, namely, the Divine Image and Likeness, or the Divine Breath. And Eve became the mother of all the living, the source of life (Genesis 3:20).

7. Reality: Illusion, Liberation, or Bondage?

Bondage and Liberation are of the mind alone.

SRI RAMAKRISHNA

Jung believed that anything that affects us becomes our reality. Dreams, imagination and fantasies, and cultural and religious myths are a manifestation of our inner reality. Self-talk creates our reality and influences the way we respond to it. It is the expression of our personal unconsciousness that is formed by our life experiences, especially those of the first six years of our lives.

In addition to our personal unconscious, Jung discovered that we are all a part of the collective unconscious. We genetically inherit the experiences and beliefs of the human race in general, especially our ancestral past. Our ethnic heritage, allegiance to a religious group, and nationality are active parts of our collective unconsciousness. This affects our worldview and the way we respond to people and situations. All of this is *My Reality*, which is subjective and personal—a reality that I guard with strong emotions. Then there is *Objective Reality*, which belongs to science. It is based on proven facts and universal principles. While we know a lot about this reality and how it works, *My Reality* often blinds us to it, making us see the world not as it is but as we are.

At the first Parliament of World Religions in 1893, Swami Vivekananda invited people to leave their personal wells and come to the ocean where we experience oneness in the Divine Essence. This invitation was to let go of *My Reality* and enter the *Mystical Reality* where we experience oneness with the Divine Essence. Swami Vivekananda believed, "All differences in this world are of degree and not of a kind because oneness is the secret of everything." He shared a hymn that he and millions of others have been praying for centuries: "As the different streams having their sources in different paths which men take through different tendencies, various though they appear, crooked or straight, all lead to Thee."

Swami Vivekananda's clarion call is still relevant for us today:

> Sectarianism, bigotry, and its horrible descendant, fanaticism, have long possessed this beautiful earth. They have filled the earth with violence, drenched it often and often with human blood, destroyed civilization, and sent whole nations to despair. Had it not been for these horrible demons, human society would be far more advanced than it is now.

The way to end all fanaticism, especially that which is driven by religion, politics, and culture, is to awaken to the *Mystical Reality*. When we experience Oneness in the Divine Essence that overflows into every part of Creation, we realize that whatever happens to one part affects the whole. This state of being does not come from chasing after gurus, socio-political ideologies, or Sacred Scriptures. The source of the Mystical Life springs forth from the depth of our being.

At the core of my being, *My Reality* is the same as *Mystical Reality*. However, unwanted thoughts and beliefs creep into our lives, like weeds or invasive species. They shroud and blur the *Mystical Reality*, being subtle and sneaky; intentionality and effort are needed to root them out. The more we awaken to the *Mystical Reality*, the more we feel liberated and experience the joy of being alive.

8. Wise Fools!

Run from what's comfortable. Forget safety. Live where you fear to live. Destroy your reputation. Be notorious. I have tried prudent planning long enough. From now on I'll be mad.

RUMI

Rumi's insightful thoughts are very challenging. Letting go of the familiarities and securities of life is a scary proposition, but amid this confusion, there is also the excitement of freedom. When we break away from the shackles of this life, we become one with nature, trusting totally in Divine Providence. Like the young eagles, we are pushed out of the comforts of the nest, only to find the wind beneath our wings and make the sky our home.

We then begin to shed our human skins that give us our religious, cultural, and political identities and instead, live by our true spiritual identities. As a spiritual being, we now flow with the rest of Creation, totally absorbed in the Universal Soul.

Rumi's words are an invitation to live the fullness of life in peace and harmony. They open the door to a deeper spiritual life and the beginning of the mystical. If we let ourselves be drawn through that door, our relationship with the Divine will gradually deepen until it explodes into total trust and we are forever drunk on Divine Love. It is then that the total acceptance and unconditional love of God becomes an experience and a celebration!

This Divine drunkenness inspires us to die while we are still alive so we can be free from our sacred golden cages—to die to the securities that come from material possessions and from cultural and religious identities. In dying, we are free from the chains of false havens and the transitory aspects of life. We burst forth and become one with a universal culture, turning religion into a dance of life that is free from creeds, theologies, and dogmas. Walls begin to crumble with the whole of creation merging into a kaleidoscope of Divine symphony. We let go of our sanctuaries and fly on the wings of the Divine Power, Presence, and Essence.

A Hindu Sanyasi, Buddhist Bhikshu, and Muslim Fakir are ascetics in the Eastern tradition who dedicate their lives to the pursuit of self-realization and God-realization in this life. They live a life of total renunciation. They all follow the commands of Jesus: "Whoever comes to me and does not hate father and mother, wife and children, brothers and sisters, yes, and even life itself, cannot be my disciple" (Luke 14:26).

Every saint was condemned as crazy before they were canonized saints. Live Rumi's madness just for a moment or a day and experience the ecstasy of Divine Love and Divine Life! Even when the ecstasy fades, its effects will sustain you on the mystical path.

9. To Question Is to Be Alive

My soul is from elsewhere, I'm sure of that,
and I intend to end up there.

RUMI

Socrates was sentenced to death for corrupting the youth. He invited them to explore the existential questions with his famous dictum: "The unexamined life is not worth living."

Unfortunately, religions and societies, with their dogmatic statements, consider critical thinking a threat to their power and the status quo. Religion has explained dogmatically the consequence of the life that we live here on Earth. And the Global North considers sickness and death a failure.

In response to Socrates' dictum, we continue to explore these existential questions: Who am I? What is the meaning of life? According to science, our bodies are made up of elements that first came from stardust that is present in every part of creation. In ancient Indian philosophy *Prana* is the life force or spirit-energy that is present in our breath and in the entire universe. When we die, our bodies will go back to the earth where they came from and our breath will continue to be part of the Universal Life Force.

Teilhard de Chardin, a Jesuit priest and famous paleontologist, believed that we are spiritual beings having a human experience, not human beings looking for a spiritual experience. He developed his theory of Cosmic Evolution and was silenced by the religious authorities.

Albert Einstein believed that the religion of the future will be a cosmic religion that will transcend a personal God and avoid dogma and theology.

10. From Being an Individual to Becoming Universal

The personal, if it is deep enough,
becomes universal, mythical, symbolic.

ANAIS NIN

In many ancient cultures, individuals were known by their tribal or clan name. Their individuality melded into the group identity. Nelson Mandela and Archbishop Tutu expressed this reality through the Ubuntu philosophy: "I am because we are!" They took Ubuntu beyond the boundaries of South Africa and invited people from all over the world to embrace Ubuntu.

We find Ubuntu in the Qur'an. "O Mankind, we created you from a single pair of male and female, and made you into nations and tribes that you may know one another" (Sura

49:13). We realize our interconnectedness by recognizing our single source. In other words, "I am because we are." The Qur'an goes further in revealing our individual and collective identity in the Divine Essence. "We have created man and know what his soul whispers to him, and We are closer to him than his jugular vein" (Sura 50:16). Jesus revealed his mission when he prayed for all of humanity: "As you, Father, are in me and I am in you, may they also be in us, so that the world may believe that you have sent me" (John 17:21).

How do we realize our Universal identity? When we see the Divine in us, we are individuals; when we see ourselves in the Divine, we become universal. As a drop in the ocean, we are individuals; when we see ourselves as the entire ocean in the drop, we become universal. The more we live in the here and now, the more we realize oneness with the Universal Divine Essence. This present moment now is part of every moment from the beginning to the end of time. Therefore, this present moment is part of eternal time. Likewise, the place where we are at any moment at all is part of the entire universe.

II. Physical Distance for Spiritual Intimacy

I do not crave intimacy that involves a touch of a hand,
but instead one that causes a flame to burn in my soul.

UNKNOWN

Physical distance and spiritual intimacy seem like a paradox, but these are key to happy and mature relationships. The way to appreciate the beauty and grandeur of a mountain is to look at it from a distance. The most beautiful paintings of a sunset are those that are absorbed from a distance and in silence. The silence between the notes makes the music of our lives. To develop and experience deep intimacy, we need physical distance and moments of silence between spouses, parents and children, teachers and students, friends, and above all, with God.

Physical distance and silence help us realize that a tree is not just a tree but a miracle. So is a mountain. Every person and all of creation is an epiphany of the Divine Essence. St. Ignatius will insist on reverential distance in the spiritual life. While you may kiss the places where the persons you are contemplating were, you do not touch the persons themselves. Ignatius believes that as we mature in the spiritual life, we will realize the Divine power, presence, and essence in every creature (Spiritual Exercises, 39). Physical distance and silence foster spiritual intimacy.

The Middle Eastern mystic Kahlil Gibran writes in *The Prophet*, "Let there be spaces in your togetherness, and let the winds of the heavens dance between you. Love one another but make not a bond of love." The only way we can be in a meaningful loving relationship with anyone, especially those who are close to us—our family, friends, and God—is by creating a sacred distance or space. Without this sacred distance, love becomes a form of bondage. Kahlil Gibran continues, "Give your hearts, but not into each other's keeping. For only the hand of Life can contain your hearts." This will help us not to suffer in times of rejection, betrayal, or the death of a loved one.

We depend on others, but we cannot be dependent on anyone, not even God, if we want to grow in intimacy. A famous Zen master, Tozan, would say, "Blue Mountain is father of White Cloud. White Cloud is son of Blue Mountain. All day long they depend on each other, without being dependent on each other. White Cloud is always White Cloud, Blue Mountain is always Blue Mountain."

12. We Are the Universe Experiencing Itself

Stop acting so small. You are the universe in ecstatic motion.

RUMI

All the elements of the Universe are in each of us. The ancient Indian philosophy captured this reality with a Sanskrit mantra, *Om So Hum*, which is translated as "I am the Universe."

We know that all the oceans are interconnected. So, if we stand in the waters of one ocean, aren't we a part of all the oceans? Similarly, the ground that I touch anywhere on earth is part of the entire universe. This present moment is part of every moment from the beginning of time and every moment till the end of time.

When we see the Divine in us, we feel small, but when we experience ourselves in the Divine, we become infinite. We feel small when we see ourselves as separate from the universe. But when we see ourselves made up of similar material as the universe, we feel great.

Our breath or our life force is part of the energy of the Universe. It existed before we were born and will continue to exist after we die. Our bodies will return to stardust and our spirits or life force will continue to exist with the Universe in ecstatic motion. Our present life is the dash between the year we were born and the day we die. We are living in the parenthesis of eternal life.

13. Take Charge of Your Mind

*Why do you stay in prison
when the door is so wide open?*

RUMI

Our brains fire the way they are wired. We come wired when we are born. The collective unconscious of our family, culture, and religion becomes an integral part of our being. Sigmund Freud believed that the way we experience the first six years of our lives sets the stage for the rest of our lives. Significant individuals and life experience define our identity. We become imprisoned by these beliefs and forget who we are in our essence: Divine.

Neuroscience, on the other hand, talks about brain plasticity. Our brains have the ability to change as a result of new experiences. We create our own thinking and have control over our minds. It is true that our past influences our present, but we can take control of the present and determine our future. The most painful thing is to be stuck and to wallow in the past.

By recognizing the gift of the present moment, we break free from the fearful anxiety of the future and the regrets of the past. When we look at nature, we do not see any stress, fear, or anxiety. Nature teaches us to flow with life and experience life in all its fullness.

PART II

Opening Up to Wisdom and Love

14. Am I Divine or a Sinner?

It is a sin to call another human a sinner.
Divinities on earth, sinners?

SWAMI VIVEKANANDA

A funeral or a wake often invites us to reflect on the existential questions: Who am I? Where do I come from? Why am I here? What happens after I die?

In the Bible, we discover that we are the Divine Breath; we are made in God's image and likeness. Hinduism teaches that we find our identity in the Divine Essence. The Divine and I are not one, but the Divine and I are not two; we find our identity in the Divine. The Qur'an notes that God is closer to us than our jugular vein.

The Scriptures are clear about our Divine identity. The myth that God breathes the Divine Breath into dust and we become living beings reflects all other myths. Science tells us that our bodies are made from stardust. So, when we die, the body will continue to be stardust, while the life-giving breath will become one with the Divine Essence that is present in every part of Creation.

Ronald Eyre, a British journalist, once interviewed a man in India. He began by asking, "How old are you?" to which the old man replied, "About eighty." Eyre was amused and said, "*About* eighty?" The man replied that he did not know his exact age. About 75 percent of people in India at that time did not have birth certificates. What an amazing way to live life—not dwelling on age because you don't really know it! Eyre continued, "Are you afraid of dying?" The old man said, "Yes. But something tells me that when the time comes for me to die, then I will not be afraid." To Eyre's final question, "What do you think will happen to you after you die?" he responded, "Now, I am an individual; after I die, I will become Universal. That is my belief."

The challenge of our present life is to realize our identity in the Divine Essence. If we sincerely make an effort to do this, we already begin to taste, experience, and cherish this process of becoming Universal, right here on Earth. This experience nourishes us to expand our horizons at all levels, both personally and collectively.

15. Enough Is Enough

He or she who knows that enough is enough
will always have enough.

LAO-TZU

In the movie *Hello, Dolly!*, Dolly Levi is heard to say, "Money, pardon the expression, is like manure. It's not worth a thing unless it's spread around, encouraging young things to grow." This is a succinct way of saying that wealth that is not shared may begin to rot and destroy our lives. The important thing is not to give our wealth away indiscriminately but rather to share it in a way that "encourages young things to grow." Wealth is not meant to be used to rescue or enable people, keeping them codependent. Nor is it meant to be used to give us a feeling that we have done something noble and good by giving it away.

Living with enough is not limited to material things but extends most especially to the religious and spiritual. As we grow in our relationship with the Divine Essence, we realize that more is less and less is more. We appreciate the wisdom of the unknown author who says, "He who buys what he does not need steals from himself." Just as we give away material things that are superfluous, we can also begin to give away religious and spiritual practices that we no longer need. We claim once again the wisdom, simplicity, and freedom of a child. The life of a little child embodies *Leela*, the Sanskrit word that is often translated as "divine play." The pure joy of a little child reflects all reality and the cosmos, which is the creative *Leela* of the Divine Essence. As we allow ourselves to participate in the dance of the Divine *Leela*, our lives become simple and mystical. We experience deep inner peace and freedom in every circumstance of our lives.

The charism and spirituality of St. Francis of Assisi can easily be seen as *Leela*, "the ability to play." Francis lived a life of simplicity and wanted his followers to trust in Divine Providence *absolutely* and become part of the Divine *Leela*. When we learn to live with enough, we will live peaceful and undisturbed lives in the midst of chaos and turmoil.

16. The Master Doesn't Seek Fulfillment

Do you have the patience to wait till your mud
settles and the water is clear?
Can you remain unmoving till the right action
arises by itself?
The Master doesn't seek fulfillment,
Not seeking, not expecting,
She is present, and can welcome all things.
Formless Nameless Essence.

LAO TZU

In life, there will be times when we are overwhelmed with unwanted troubles and pain, feeling the stress and chaos of life's challenges. The more we struggle, the more we can get entangled in the web of anxiety, anger, or depression. During these times, we learn a lesson from muddy waters. If left alone, the mud slowly but surely settles down to the bottom, bringing more and more clarity as we look into that water. We begin to see the reflection of the sun, the moon, the stars, and the whole of creation in all its divine grandeur. We see ourselves in our essence, just as we are, as the Divine Image and Likeness, the Divine Breath! We experience the Divine Presence in every fiber of our being and every moment of our lives.

Stress has tremendous gifts. It is an invitation to be centered and become more resilient. During these stressful times, our inner being is drawn to connect with people who care about us and to reach out to others in their pain. When we allow ourselves to feel part of broken humanity, we begin to live more peacefully and effectively; even our bodies begin to rejuvenate. They say that stress never harms us, but our attitude toward stress does!

Carl Jung believed that "In all chaos there is a cosmos, in all disorder a secret order" (*The Archetypes and the Collective Unconscious*). Chaos, therefore, is an invitation to live a more authentic life, becoming more and more our true selves. We realize that we are part of the cosmos, and the cosmos is in our essence. Imitating the sage, we detach ourselves from the outcome of our chaotic life and welcome all things just as they are. We stand back, surrender our chaos to the Universe, and watch "muddy water become clear," giving birth to a dancing star.

"Be still, and know that I am God" (Psalm 46:10) is an effective way to live the life of the sages. If we anchor ourselves in deep inner peace, then we will see the face of the Divine emerging from conflicting situations in the form of realizations and inspiration. We naturally accept and flow with every moment of life.

17. Are You a Spiritual Predator or a Real Person?

It's like there is this predator energy
on this planet, and this predator energy
feeds on the essence of the spirit.

JOHN TRUDELL

It's a strange question, but one worth pondering. A predator is one who looks for other people or things in order to use, control, or harm them in some way. The worst predator is the one who does this in the name of God and religion. These predators are those who preach the prosperity gospel. In the name of God and in exchange for donations they encourage people to indulge in the material things of this world and the pleasures of life to find the meaning of their lives and the source of their happiness. Others pursue honor or power. In the process, these people not only hurt others but harm themselves in a deep way.

In the Eastern tradition, wealth and pleasure are not only good but necessary to experience the fullness of life. The key is finding the right balance or knowing what is enough. When our basic material needs are sufficiently met, we can pursue the ultimate goal of our lives: being totally immersed in intimacy with the Divine.

Similarly, pleasure is the gateway to the mystical world. At the end of our lives, we will be judged on the legitimate pleasures of life we did not enjoy (Jerusalem Talmud: Kiddushin 4:12). Pleasure is the antithesis of stress, jealousy, hatred, envy, and all negative energy that works as a slow poison within us.

Real people are not perfect, and perfect people are not real. Real people realize their identity in the Divine Essence and experience the interconnectedness with all of life; that which affects one of us affects the rest of us. They do not get lost in gender, race, nationality, or religion but connect with the Divine in everyone and in every part of Creation. Schizophrenics, alcoholics, and criminals do not exist. Rather, real people see persons who have the illnesses of schizophrenia or alcoholism or persons with criminal tendencies. Real people slowly transition from that which is transient to that which is Eternal, from the anthropomorphic God to a Cosmic Eternal Divinity.

18. Compassion without Being Attached to the Outcome

Detachment does not mean non-involvement.
You can be deeply involved and not entangled.

SADGURU

The quest for happiness is universal. In every age, people have been trying to find happiness in the material things of this world and the pleasures of life. For some, happiness lies in the legacy of all that they accomplish and the impact they leave on life for future generations. Every culture, society, and religion offers ways of being happy.

True and lasting happiness cannot be experienced in isolation because all of life is interdependent. In fact, the happiness of one depends on the happiness of all, and the happiness of all depends on the happiness of one. This universal experience of happiness comes with compassion, without being attached to the outcome.

Living a life of compassion without being attached to the outcome is not a method but a way of life. We open ourselves to become effective channels for the Universe to affect the lives of people and the world. We let go of our ego and flow with the rhythm of life.

We find examples of genuine compassion in every major religion. Jesus introduced us to the God of compassion through the parable of the Prodigal Son. The younger brother in this parable indulged in the pleasures of life to find happiness. The older brother dedicated his life to being a dutiful son and was far from happy. He seemed self-absorbed and lacked meaningful relationships with others. The father in this parable was the epitome of compassion. He lived a life of unconditional love.

The Qur'an offers us an experience of the unfathomable compassion of God: 113 out of 114 chapters of the Qur'an begin with *Bi-Ism-i—Allah al-Rahman*, "In the name of God-Compassion!" *Al-Rahman* is not an adjective or a characteristic of God but the essence. It is also the essence of every human being.

One of the paths toward Self-Realization or God-Realization in Hinduism is *Nishkama Karma*. This is action performed without any expectation or attachment to the fruits or results. *Nishkama Karma* eliminates our ego-driven feeling of separateness and awakens our Oneness with the whole of Creation. What we do for others, we actually do for ourselves, because we are all interconnected.

Buddhism offers the *Brahmaviharas* as a path to experiencing inner peace and freedom. *Brahmaviharas* literally means the Divine Abode. One goes through four stages to experience the ultimate goal of life. The first stage is Loving Kindness, where we reach out to the people in need that *we* want to help. The second stage is Compassion, where life draws us to people in need. In this stage, we do not have control over who these people are, how long we will be in this situation, or the price we will have to pay. The third stage is Empathetic Joy. Now we rejoice in the success and happiness of others, irrespective of whether they are our friends or our competitors. The final stage is Equanimity. This does not mean indifference but a complete openness to experience. In this stage, one is totally immersed in life without being affected by reactions of love and hate, success and failure. It is a life of balance born out of wisdom. Equanimity has a balance that empowers loving kindness even in times when the people we love or reach out to do self-destructive things. It frees us from imposing our idea of happiness on the world rather than staying connected and loving with things as they are.

Living a life of true compassion enables parents to let go of the outcomes of their children, teachers of their students, and social workers, health care workers, and anyone giving aid of whomever they are helping. Living a life of compassion without being attached to the outcome reflects spiritual maturity.

True compassion has the ability to sing, "Nobody knows the trouble I've seen; nobody knows my sorrow," and with the same breath burst out confidently, "Glory, Hallelujah!"

19. Barriers to Experiencing Love

Your task is not to seek for love, but merely to
seek and find all the barriers within yourself
that you have built against it.

RUMI

I have been reflecting on some of the barriers within myself
that have kept me from experiencing love. As a little child, I
was given the formula for JOY: put Jesus first, Others next,
and Yourself last. I was taught that for God to love me, I
had to sacrifice myself for others and discount myself. The
paradox was that the more I sacrificed myself for others, the
more I struggled to feel God's love. I experienced a feeling
of being constantly judged and abandoned by God, being
rejected and condemned by the very people I sacrificed
myself for every day. I could not do enough for others to
earn God's love, and I hated myself more and more. This
was one of the biggest and strongest barriers I have had to
work on to allow Love to come in.

The need for love was so desperate that I cried out to
God, "Take away all my talents [and I was aware that they
were many] and give me one person who will love me for
myself." God sent me the only person who could love me for
myself: me. Once I began to recognize, appreciate, and celebrate myself with all my many and beautiful God-given gifts,
Love found a way to penetrate the depths of my being. This
love overflowed into the lives of people without discriminat-
ing between friend or foe, good or bad, and without counting
the cost or keeping a record. God became more and more the
Loving Living Absolute in my life.

I realized that God did not create junk but made me Important-Precious-Beautiful. That I was God's own image and likeness and the Divine Breath (Genesis 1 and 2). The more I love myself and celebrate my life by enjoying legitimate pleasures, the more I experience the abundance of true love and the more I grow in my relationship with the Absolute.

My prayer now gives God the greatest glory: "All generations will call me blessed; for the Mighty One has done great things for me" (Luke 1:48–49).

20. To Give and Not to Count the Cost

We can only give away to others
what we have inside ourselves.

WAYNE DYER

Many of us have been raised by maxims like "It is more blessed to give than to receive." "Give till it hurts." "It is in giving that we receive." Or "Give without expecting anything in return." When these maxims are taken literally, they become barriers to receiving love.

Culture and religion sometimes make receiving a sign of weakness and a negative quality. Women often martyr themselves for their children, their families, and the rest of the world. It is so difficult for them to accept the loving acknowledgment of their children, especially the little ones, during their sad and difficult times. Men have to be the strong ones and cannot show weakness. Therefore, they withdraw into their caves or go out with their buddies to escape receiving consolation from those that society has labeled as the weaker ones.

The secret to selfless giving and selfless living, I believe, is to allow ourselves to receive love. The challenge of a loving relationship is not to love but to allow ourselves to be loved. The only love we can truly give to the world is the love we have allowed ourselves to receive. All other love becomes selfish manipulation and will come back to haunt us. We end up feeling dejected and lament, "After all I have done, is this what I get in return?"

One of the effective ways I have discovered to remove the barriers to experiencing love is this: at the end of each day, rather than asking myself what more I could have given or done for others, it is more fruitful to ask: What is it that people and life were trying to give me that I did not pay attention to? I then allow myself to receive these gifts with a grateful heart. And if I am aware of the love that came to me that day, I remember it also with gratitude every night before I fall asleep. Falling asleep with gratitude in my heart will make my unconscious a pool of gratitude and increase my capacity for receiving love. This love, of course, will overflow into life without my even knowing it.

21. Find Your Internal Anchor

Feelings come and go like clouds in a windy sky.
Conscious breathing is my anchor.

THICH NHAT HANH

People who have been rejected or abused as children and have experienced loneliness have been given this advice for finding love: "Give love instead of asking for it." "Stop crying about being rejected and feeling unloved and lonely. This is being self-centered." "Find someone who is sick and alone and reach out to them without expecting thanks. This way you will begin to feel a sense of satisfaction simply because you have been selfless." This kind of advice seems to come from people who do not know what it is like to live with traumatic memories. And those who try to follow this advice only create stronger barriers to receiving love.

My experience has been that we cannot give what we do not have. We need to find ways of learning to love ourselves and stop trying to live by the rules set by others. We must avoid thoughts such as "I must be loved and appreciated by everyone, otherwise I am worthless." What changed me was a mantra that was given to me: *I AM IMPORTANT–PRECIOUS–BEAUTIFUL.* Even if others dislike me or criticize me, and whether I succeed or fail, my essence cannot change: *IMPORTANT–PRECIOUS–BEAUTIFUL.* I began to reflect on this mystery and the reality of who I am. I repeated this mantra like an unbroken recitation, when things were going well and when they were not. This mantra sank into my unconscious. Every night as I fell asleep, I recited my mantra, allowing it to sink into my unconscious.

This mantra sprung forth from the depth of my being with the first conscious moments every morning and permeated every moment of my day. I slowly began to appreciate myself more and more and allowed myself to receive love: not only love that came to me in the moment, but love that was offered to me throughout my life. Slowly but surely my love began to overflow into my relationships, my work, and every aspect of my life. My capacity for receiving and giving love keeps growing.

Every time I feel unloved or unloving, all I have to do is to withdraw and breathe in consciously: *IMPORTANT–PRECIOUS–BEAUTIFUL.*

22. Giving without Receiving Can Be Suicidal

In ordinary life, we hardly realize that we receive a great deal more than we give, and that it is only with gratitude that life becomes rich.

DIETRICH BONHOEFFER

During the time of his conversion, St. Ignatius tells us that while he was reading the *Lives of the Saints*, he had a burning desire to imitate the saints. He contemplated surpassing the saints in their heroism and austerities. He fasted frequently and scourged himself to make up for his past sins. His penance gave him a deep abhorrence of those sins, but he did not feel forgiven or loved by God. This in turn created tormenting scruples that became mental and spiritual torture.

The more he increased his penance, the less peace and love he experienced.

Ignatius lived in the Dominican monastery and prayed seven hours a day, scourged himself several times a day, and helped others who were sick and in need. But the more he gave of himself, the emptier and more desperate he felt— to the point that he even wanted to kill himself. He finally gave up, surrendered totally to God, and kept his focus on God alone. In his openness to God, he began to experience and receive many mystical graces that had been there all the time. Trying to earn God's love had become the very obstacle to receiving and experiencing love.

Divine gifts cannot be earned. If we truly believe, with Paul (Romans 8:17), that we are children of God and therefore heirs to the Divine, then the gifts of God are not only our privilege but our right. They are ours—free to be experienced and to be experienced freely.

Reflecting on this part of Ignatius' life, we realize that giving without receiving is prone to suicide: mental, emotional, spiritual, and sometimes even physical.

23. Service Is Joy

*I dreamt and saw that life was joy. I awoke and saw that
life was service. I acted and behold, service was joy.*
RABINDRANATH TAGORE

India has a rich spiritual tradition of service. Service is an effective means to find one's own authentic self. In many spiritual and mystical traditions, the Divine resides in the heart of every part of Creation. Therefore, service is often seen as worship of the Divine. Swami Vivekananda reiterated this reality in his famous quote: "It is a privilege to serve mankind, for this is the worship of God. God is here, in all these human souls. He is the soul of man."

A nun in India who worked in a leper colony was once asked what inspired her to keep nursing people with leprosy. Her spontaneous response was that she worshiped the Divine Image and Likeness in each of her patients. It was her path to intimacy and union with the Divine.

St. Ignatius of Loyola demonstrates the stages he went through in his service of God. He began by working *for* God. He imitated the saints in their external behavior without integrating their inner spiritual strength. This often left him empty and even led him to temptations of suicide. Once he surrendered and let the Divine work in and through him, he began to work *with* God and to feel equal to but separate from those he served. As he grew in his intimacy with the Divine, he began working in communion with the Divine and experienced the people he served as intimate companions.

The growth in serving others is closely related to our own spiritual growth. St. Ignatius reflects this through the prayer methods he suggests in the Spiritual Exercises. He introduces us to Meditation. In this method, we use the three powers of the soul: memory, understanding, and the will. We call to memory the words of Scripture and understand it with our minds and intellect. We then make resolutions. In this stage of our spiritual life, we choose the people we are going to serve, how long we will serve them, and the price we are willing to pay. Our service is working *for* people and *for* God.

Ignatian prayer then moves to Contemplation: we open ourselves to the mystery and to life, which in turn allows the mystery to transform us into the mystery. In this prayer, we become what we contemplate. In this form of service, we open ourselves to anyone who needs us, and we have no control over the price we will have to pay. In the contemplative stage, we work with the people we serve and we become one with them.

The final stage of Ignatian prayer is the Application of the Senses. In this prayer, we are totally one with the Divine and the mystery of life. In our experience of comingling with the Divine, we become intimate and totally one with the people we serve. In serving others, we find our true selves. Serving others is the best worship of the Divine.

Jesus spells out the meaning of service by his words and example. His commandment "Love your neighbor as yourself" invites us to experience the interconnectedness of life. It also reminds us that the Divine Essence is present in every part of Creation. Therefore, service of others is true worship of the Divine. Jesus deepens this reality by his example at the Last Supper. In washing the feet of his disciples, he demonstrated how service is a means of communion with the Divine and the people we serve. He reprimanded Simon Peter, who refused to allow Jesus to wash his feet. "Unless I wash you," Jesus told him, "you have no share with me" (John 13:8).

Rumi believes that "When you do things from your soul, you feel a river moving in you, a joy."

24. Receive Before You Give Away

Everything comes to us that belongs to us
if we create the capacity to receive it.

RABINDRANATH TAGORE

The Universe has infinite gifts that are available to anyone who knows how to receive them in order to share them. The human soul is capable of receiving infinite gifts. If a human only wants to receive the gifts of the Universe, a time will come when these gifts overwhelm and destroy the individual. And if the individual just keeps giving away the gifts of the Universe without appreciating and relishing them, the individual will soon feel desolate and empty.

The gifts of the Universe are unconditional and are available to anyone and everyone. These gifts are all present within us and are unique resources needed to fulfill the purpose of our lives. We need to trust that everything we need is reachable within us. When these gifts come knocking, we must be willing to open the door.

There are those who will not accept these gifts just because they are not aware of them or because they do not feel worthy. Others selfishly hold on to these gifts to boost their egotistical and arrogant selves. We need to ask ourselves how we are using these gifts. Are we working toward building a better world or selfishly destroying it?

The challenge of our relationship with the Universe is to receive its gifts *and* to share them with others to build and harmonize all of creation. Besides, the only gifts we truly own are those we have given away or shared.

25. Forgiving Ourselves

Forgive those who hurt you,
but never forget what it taught you.

JOSHUA DOWIDAT

We only forgive when there is nothing to forgive. When we let go of hurts and resentments, we receive gifts from the painful experiences of our lives. When we forgive, we break the fetters that keep us from enjoying the fullness of life, affect our self-worth, and block our vision of our true essence. It opens a window that offers a glimpse of the Divine Essence and Power within us.

In Hebrew, one of the words for forgiveness is *nasa*, which means to carry away. Just as NASA (The National Aeronautics and Space Administration USA) develops shuttles that carry people and cargo to outer space, when we forgive, we surrender our resentments, hurts, and pains to the Universe. Forgiving others is easier than receiving forgiveness or forgiving ourselves. But forgiving ourselves for those things that we were not responsible for is something we seldom think about.

Imagine the movie of your life. From the time you were born, you experienced joys, trauma, love, and pain. Psychologists say the experiences of the first six years of our lives have an impactful influence on how we live our lives. So, from birth through every stage of our lives, we are bombarded with experiences that affect us: those teenage years when we felt lost trying to find ourselves, relationships that were hurtful through no fault of our own, or times when we got sick. Lovingly offer yourself *nasa* at every stage. Allow the Cosmic world to sweep you away and carry you to where we break up into stardust and experience healing and wholeness once again.

It is good to forgive and not to forget! We should remember the people and life experiences we have forgiven as a way of protecting ourselves from getting hurt in similar situations. It also makes us less likely to hurt others because we remember the pain it will cause them. Above all, as long as we remember, we will continue to empower ourselves and others.

26. From Brokenness to Wholeness

The wound is the place where the Light enters you.

RUMI

Pain is a fact of life and an opportunity to experience purification and enlightenment. It is in the nature of life to break us physically, emotionally, and spiritually. Every one of us has probably had times when life seemed hard and unimaginable. In those unbearable times, if we open ourselves to seek Divine intervention, we realize the Divine power abides within us. Every wound carves a deeper path to this Divine source within us. The deeper we travel in our inner Divine space, the more we realize that the power within us is aligned with the power and the energy of the Universe.

The gift that brokenness offers us is a better understanding of ourselves, others, and life itself. It gives us a heart filled with compassion. Our brokenness breaks down the barriers that our ego and arrogance have built: barriers in the name of religion, culture, and politics. Our brokenness purifies us of our prejudice and gives us an insight into the truth. Truth, for Mahatma Gandhi, was finding our identity in the Divine Essence and experiencing the interconnectedness of all Creation.

27. Suffering Is a Choice

If you cry because the sun has gone out of your life,
your tears will prevent you from seeing the stars.
RABINDRANATH TAGORE

The Buddhists believe that pain is a fact of life; suffering is a choice. When someone is diagnosed with a disease that sounds like a death sentence, it is painful. If we resist that pain, it will become suffering. Unless we are able to move beyond the pain, we make the choice to focus only on the devastation of the disease and its negative effects. We wallow in self-pity and hopelessness, which can be as devastating as the disease itself. However, after we have processed and experienced the stages of grief—namely, denial, anger, bargaining, depression, and finally acceptance—we may then begin to look at the gift that this disease offers. We begin to live as we have never lived before. With a short time to live, we have little time for anger, hatred, or jealousy. We may slip back into self-pity from time to time, but then we pull ourselves up, looking for the gifts that life offers, and begin to appreciate the many things that we took for granted, especially our near and dear ones.

Our understanding of the world in the "sunshine" of normality is often viewed through the lens of our prejudices and past experiences. However, in the "darkness" of painful events, we have the chance to experience life in truth and objectivity. We are no longer influenced by the lenses through which we view the world. It is in moments of darkness that we are given the opportunity to pause and choose our response. We may not be able to change our external circumstances, but we have power over our attitude to life's challenges. Pain that is not resisted purifies and enlightens us. It allows us to see the stars.

In times of genuine pain, through the tears in our eyes, we will find the rainbow in our hearts. Those painful tears will unwrap the gift of life's wisdom that will help us live a more authentic and fuller life. We realize that pain can break our bodies and even affect our mental and emotional life, but it cannot touch our Divine Essence. When we live from our core, we begin to let go of our attachments. This is the only way to truly enjoy people, places, and things in our lives.

Not all experiences of pain are physical. A breakup in a relationship is also very painful. The pain is even deeper when the person we trusted enough to share the depth of our personal life with cheats on us, deserts us, or dies. If we don't resist this pain but allow it to enlighten us, this experience allows us to realize that when someone loves us, they do not make us happy. They make us aware of the source of our happiness that is deep within us. So, a breakup in a relationship is painful, but no one can touch the source of our happiness. Similarly, an economic or financial crisis might be painful, but we have an opportunity to become aware of the superfluous things in our lives that we can do without.

It also helps us simplify our lives and get rid of clutter. This in turn makes space for spiritual growth.

There was a Jesuit in India who was in a motorcycle accident in Mumbai. His right leg was broken in many places, which left him in chronic and sometimes throbbing pain for thirty years. He was an architect who designed schools and churches. For him, these buildings were sermons in stone. They expressed the charism and spirituality of the ones running these institutions. His broken leg did not stop him from traversing the country sharing his gifts—not only his architecture, but also his deep spirituality. When he was asked how he dealt with his chronic pain, his response was that pain was all in the mind. If he had spent his time on his physical pain, he might not have had the energy to live his life's purpose. His architecture and spiritual conversations remain his legacy, long after his death at the age of ninety-one. Pain is a fact of life; suffering is a choice.

28. Capturing a Slice of Life, Freezing a Moment in Time

In one drop of water are found all the secrets of the oceans; in one aspect of you are found all the aspects of existence.

KAHLIL GIBRAN

I am still wondering how I landed in the paradise of Maui, one of the Hawaiian Islands. While I was there, I took a tour bus to Hana. They say that the road has about six hundred curves and sixty bridges. We were told at the onset that this trip was all about the journey, not the destination. At one point, we stopped at a waterfall. Some of the group got out to swim in the big waterfall; I was alone at the lower, smaller waterfall. After I waded knee-deep through the freezing water, I sat on a rock to dry my legs and enjoy this revitalizing experience. At that moment, a young woman came to the waterfall. She asked me if the water was cold; I said it was freezing but very refreshing.

She came out of the water after an invigorating swim and playfully splashed some cold water on me. We then stood and talked for a bit. When she said that she had attended a course on Taoism in San Francisco and was into yoga, I realized that this woman was on a spiritual quest. I mentioned one of my father's wisdom sayings: "Enough is Abundance." She became very still and reverently repeated the phrase a few times. "Enough is Abundance." She was deeply moved, and I was touched. She said she felt like she was Siddhartha who had just found the Buddha. We said goodbye and she pointed to the camper she had rented and was driving without any particular destination. Yes, she was on a spiritual quest.

Within an hour I had forgotten what this woman looked like, but I had captured a slice of life; that moment in time is now frozen forever. As I continued on the tour bus, I was in a daze. I wasn't sure if this person was real or had come to visit me from the spirit world. I can still recall the amazing sunsets, the full moon and its reflection on the ocean, and so many other moments of beauty from the trip. As time goes on, I may not be able to recall them, but the effect will linger in me.

29. Doing Nothing

Doing nothing is better than
being "busy" doing nothing.

LAO TZU

How often after a busy day do we find ourselves wondering if we achieved anything significant? By the end of such days, we feel tired, frustrated, and empty. It seems like we were busy doing nothing.

Doing nothing is the art of flowing with life and living the way of nature. When we plan our day and then allow the Great Spirit to be the rudder that navigates our day, the life force flows out of us, inadvertently getting things done. When this happens, the singer stops singing, allowing the song to rise up from the depths of their being; the painting flows out of the artist; and the dancer and the dance become one.

Children live this natural way of flowing with the rhythm of life. So do Indian villagers who do not have birth certificates. They focus on the mystery of each moment instead of dwelling on age, the past, and the future. This is living testimony of the philosophy (often attributed to Abraham Lincoln) that "In the end, it's not the years in your life that counts. It's the life in your years." Indigenous tribes in different parts of the world are also closely connected with nature and flow with the rhythm of life. A ninety-year-old man prayed to God to find out the purpose of the rest of his life. The response he received was intriguing: *Your life will have a purpose, but you will not know it and you will fulfill that purpose without knowing it!*

30. Our Teacher, the Butterfly

*The butterfly counts not months
but moments, and has time enough.*

RABINDRANATH TAGORE

The key to live the fullness of life is to live the "I," now and here. The "I" is our essence that never changes, not the "me" that is in constant flux. Living in the present moment and place is to experience what is real. The past is gone; the future is not yet here.

Living in the moment, like the butterfly, is to have all the time in the world. Being happy with enough is to have the abundance of life. The butterfly is a witness that it is more important to live a quality of life and not crave more days.

31. Every Translation Is an Interpretation

*Silence is the language of God;
all else is poor translation.*

RUMI

Silence is not the absence of noise but an inner stillness. It is the eye of a storm or the depth of a turbulent ocean. It is living fully in the moment. Silence is not total concentration, but total concentration is silence. When we give ourselves fully to any activity, however mundane, we silence the "monkey mind" and experience absolute stillness. The fragrance of this inner silence will then permeate all our external activities.

The soul of Nature is silence; when we immerse ourselves in Nature, we find a channel to the tranquility at the core of our being where we encounter eternal peace and utter bliss. We do not have a practice of silence; we *become* silence. This experience surpasses sound and goes deeper than the knowledge of the five senses. It also transcends our physical, mental, and emotional pain. Silence is not a denial of pain. Being fully aware of the pain, without identifying with it, helps us live the fullness of life.

Those who are rooted in silence communicate words that reflect the Divine Essence that abides in the sanctuary at the core of our being. When we experience the miracle of life in silence, everyone around us will feel the effects.

PART III

Living with Purpose, Peace, and Joy

32. Intuition: Key to Living Your Life Purpose

Life is a series of natural and spontaneous changes. Don't resist them—that only creates sorrow. Let reality be reality. Let things flow naturally forward in whatever way they like.

LAO TZU

Intuition is unlearned knowledge and innate wisdom. It is the manifestation of Divine Consciousness within us. In ancient spiritual traditions, intuition is a direct and spontaneous connection with the mind of the Universe. Mystics like St. Ignatius of Loyola believe that intuition is the most common and surest way of realizing our true path at every moment of our lives (Spiritual Exercises, 175). However, the knowledge of the mind and the feelings in our hearts are learned and can often muddle the flow of our authentic lives.

Intuition is the highest and purest form of consciousness. It is still and quiet, experienced in the silence between thoughts, words, and deeds. Mahatma Gandhi called intuition

59

the "Little Voice" that speaks in silence. As he led India in the struggle for independence, he observed every Monday as a day of silence. He wanted to be attuned to the Little Voice, his intuition. It was this experience that he was reflecting on when he wrote: "There come to us moments in life when about some things we need no proof from without. A little voice within us tells us, "You are on the right track. Move neither to your left nor right, but keep to the straight and narrow way."

Pause to think about the relationships and careers you chose that you now regret. Through honest introspection, you will recognize that your intuition had raised red flags that were smothered by the logic of the mind and the feelings of the heart. The mind and the heart are both seductive and hypnotic. One of the common regrets of the dying is that they wished they had lived the life they were destined to live. Reboot your life now, without any regret about the past or anxiety about the future. It is never too late to claim your personal destiny. The past influences your present, but it cannot control your present and determine your future; those controls are in your hands! Step into the natural flow of life.

33. Am I an Echo or a Wave?

Be a voice not an echo. UNKNOWN

Is my life steered by my personal convictions, or am I bound by the dictates of another? Am I an echo living someone else's truth or a wave that flows with the Ocean of Life and whose essence is Spiritual and Divine?

Socrates chose death over blindly following the decrees of his religious elders. In his reflection that the unexamined life is not worth living, he reminds us that a healthy critical mind is indispensable to living an authentic and meaningful life.

We must continue to develop our personal convictions while always being open to a greater reality. The Buddha's last words before he died were "Be lamps unto yourselves. Rely on yourselves, and do not rely on external help." Humans are ultimately responsible for their own destiny and inner bliss.

Every human being has an inner voice, the voice of the Great Spirit. It gives power, inner freedom, and an experience of the interconnectedness of life. Through his experiments with Truth, Mahatma Gandhi believed that "Everyone who wills can hear the inner voice. It is within everyone....There come to us moments in life when about some things we need no proof from without."

The inner voice and the Truth we experience deep within us will always find a spontaneous and irrepressible expression. In the words of W.H. Auden,

> All I have is a voice
> To undo the folded lie,
> The romantic lie in the brain
> Of the sensual man-in-the-street
> And the lie of Authority
> Whose buildings grope the sky.
>
> (SEPTEMBER 1, 1939)

Auden's poem, written prior to World War II, was describing Hitler's propaganda machine, which had a brazen disregard for the truth and controlled how reality was perceived. If an idea is repeated often enough, it is taken as true. And since there was no easy way to fact-check at the time, Hitler's hate-filled rhetoric, vile determination of the inequality of races, and perfect authority of the Führer were believed as fact.

Interestingly, leading newspapers in New York published this poem in its entirety in the wake of September 11, 2001. The poem sounds the warning sirens before fateful moments in history when whole nations will succumb to the manipulative rhetoric of dictators to bend people to their will.

Therefore, we need to be listening to the inner voice and building our lives based on its promptings. This requires constant vigilance and alertness to the silent whispers of the Spirit deep within us. We need courage to be a part of the wave that will eventually take us to the Ocean of Love and Divine Life. This is the call of Jesus to all:

> Enter through the narrow gate; for the gate is wide and the road is easy that leads to destruction, and there are many who take it. For the gate is narrow and the road is hard that leads to life, and there are few who find it. + MATTHEW 7:13-14

34. Divine Flea

That's a valiant flea that dares eat
his breakfast on the lip of a lion.

WILLIAM SHAKESPEARE

Sojourner Truth lived as a slave from the age of nine. Her slave name was Isabella; she was sold several times until she was ultimately sold to John Dumont. Like all her other previous owners, Dumont beat Isabella, and his wife, Sally, sexually abused her. Isabella found solace by building a little shrine in the woods with some twigs and branches, an African tradition she may have learned from her mother. Over the years, she developed an intimate relationship with the Divine. After toiling for fourteen years, moved by Divine inspiration, Isabella ran away with her daughter Sophia.

As a runaway slave, she joined the Second Great Awakening, a Protestant evangelical movement where people lived a simple life by the promptings of the Holy Spirit. She soon became an inspirational speaker and challenged people through her unique interpretation of the Bible as a woman and a former slave. Her longing for some structure and family lured her to be spellbound by the "Prophet Matthias" who, intimidated by her charisma, often beat her, making her feel like a slave again.

In 1843, Isabella had a foundational spiritual experience that would change her life forever and give her total inner freedom. On the day of Pentecost, she left New York under a new name, Sojourner Truth, free from slavery and the abusive structures of religion. She continued being an inspirational speaker, fighting for the emancipation of slaves, freedom for the Black community, and the rights of all women. Her faith and preaching introduced her to abolition-ists and women's rights crusaders. Frederick Douglass, the abolitionist, admired her speaking ability but looked upon her as an uncultured person. When he called upon Blacks to work for their freedom using force, Sojourner Truth con-fronted him with the famous words "Is God gone?" She was the champion of nonviolence and the belief in God's power to overcome injustice and oppression.

Throughout her life she refused to "keep her place." With her faith anchored in the Divine, she became a force to be reckoned with and was determined not to be intimidated or ignored. When a slave owner sneered at her, proclaiming that he did not care for her anti-slavery talk any more than he would for the bite of a flea, Sojourner Truth's sponta-neous response was "Lord willing I'll keep you scratching!"

Deep within every one of us is the Divine Flea that con-stantly goads us toward comingling with the Divine Essence. If we keep ourselves attuned to the movements of the Divine Flea, we will realize more and more our own Divine Essence. As a result, in the very depth of our being, we will enjoy bliss, freedom, and peace which cannot be touched by any external forces. The Divine Flea within each one of us will keep our friends and family, our religious and social groups forever scratching and restless for deep inner freedom and craving for the fullness of life.

Her assumed name, Sojourner Truth, also reminds us that life is a journey and our quest for truth is relentless. Her relationship with the Divine that began at the shrine she built in the woods moved through the oppressive struc-tures of religion and came full circle to the Higher Power, the Divine Spirit of the Universe.

35. Building a Better World for Future Generations

Don't be satisfied with stories, how things have gone with others. Unfold your own myth.

RUMI

Everyone writes their own life story and lives out the plot. According to Carl Jung, we all have a personal unconscious, and we are all part of the collective unconscious. We inherit the knowledge, wisdom, and experience of the groups we belong to: our families, religions, cultures, and the human community as a whole. From the time we are born, our personal life experiences become our personal storyline and the plot we live out the rest of our lives.

Most people live the stories that come from the collective unconscious. If we do not critically examine our personal and collective stories, we will only strengthen the plot and pass it on to the next generation. How do we change a world that seems to be chaotic and sharply polarized? Whatever we do, it is important to pay attention to the purity of our motivation and our thoughts.

They say that thought is energy that we put out into the universe. This energy affects the collective unconscious. If our reaction to what happens in the world is one of anger, hatred, anxiety, or fear, our collective unconscious becomes more rooted in negative energy. But we can always edit our storyline and recalculate the plot trajectory. We are the star, the hero, and the director of our own movie. If we begin to respond to our world positively, we will overwrite the negative energy.

Sometimes songs with positive lyrics can help in changing the world: songs like "Imagine," sung by John Lennon. Or USA for Africa "We are the World." We need to listen to the lyrics of these or similar songs until we understand the words, believe in the reality of these words, and let them sink into our personal unconscious. Slowly but surely, we will transform the world and offer a more hopeful and positive collective unconscious to the next generation.

36. Life Is a Pilgrimage, Not a Destination

A journey becomes a pilgrimage as we discover, day by day, that the distance traveled is less important than the experience gained.

ERNEST KURTZ

Life is more than a journey; it is a pilgrimage. A journey has an end and a destination, but a pilgrim keeps moving along or dies. For a pilgrim, there is always more of life and infinite possibilities. The pilgrim is on a quest to realize his or her true self and the meaning of life. The mystery and adventure never end.

At the beginning of the pilgrimage, we might need the eyes of another to see the wonders of this universe, the heart of one who loves us to experience the inner depths of the mystery of life, and the soul of a beloved to live the fullness of life as a true mystic. It is with love of the other that we discover the delights and the deeper mysteries of life. Each climax in life points to another that is sometimes different, often unfamiliar and deeper. Each boundary is the beginning of another horizon.

The path of the pilgrim is often challenging and inspiring at the same time. Every new knowledge expands the horizons in search of a deeper meaning of life.

The pilgrim has to constantly respond to the demands for infinite adjustments, while facing fears of the unknown and uncertainties about the ultimate goal. Sometimes the pilgrim will be surrounded by crowds of other pilgrims. The pilgrim might even find a soulmate. However, in the end, the pilgrim is detached from everyone and is always alone.

If we focus on the path, we will truly live life in all its fullness and experience the joys and the miracles of life. We will notice the little seeds that turn into plants and sometimes into big, magnificent trees. We will share the wonder of seeing a caterpillar turn into a beautiful butterfly. We will celebrate the seasons changing as each one manifests the shades and moods of life's mystery and glory. The night sky will open up glorious worlds that we never noticed before. The song of the bird, the sound of the waves, and the gentle caress of the wind will transform and transport us into a magical and mystical world. We will never experience all this if we obsess about our destination.

The journey of life is an adventure, and the path can sometimes, if not often, be a risky one. The path of a pilgrim is uncharted and is traversed but once. It has no traditions and no structures to guide or even support us on this pilgrim pathway of life.

It is important for the pilgrim to focus on discovering the true self. Every experience on the path nourishes and challenges us to keep exploring new horizons. A pilgrim cannot cling to any experience, however spiritual or mystical.

37. Source of True Happiness and the Meaning of Life

Clouds come floating into my life, no longer to carry rain or usher storm, but to add color to my sunset sky.

RABINDRANATH TAGORE

Clouds signify the impermanence of life, and yet they give us a glimpse of life one slice at a time. Clouds are like a natural Rorschach test; they help us project our true inner selves. We express our philosophy of life in our response to the clouds that float through the sky. Dissatisfaction and suffering in life come from running after or clinging to the transient things in life—material things, careers or status, and even family and friends.

There is life beyond the ever-changing clouds. When we identify ourselves with the sky, we experience that which never changes. We can peacefully and blissfully watch the clouds, the impermanent things in life, go by. We realize the futility of chasing after success, social status, and material possessions. We become aware that nothing is permanent. As the colors of the sky change, so do our thoughts, moods, and purpose of existence. We need to look beyond family and friends to find true meaning in life.

Time is also an illusion. Looking up at the sky and clouds reinforces the necessity of living a meaningful life. We are inspired to begin living eternal life in the here and now. As we become more mature in life, we view adversity and challenges as opportunities to grow in wisdom. We see the silver lining in every cloud. We develop the ability to make distinctions between existence and living. Existence is part of a journey. For something to exist, there needs to be an exclusive space. Material things and even thoughts take up space and keep everything else out. Existence tends to put down roots wherever it can. Living, on the other hand, is part of the pilgrimage. It accepts life fully in the moment—the good and the bad, the joyful and the painful—without clinging. These are the clouds that keep floating in and out of our lives. The pilgrim is anchored in the sky, in the never-changing, eternal reality.

In the gospels, Mary is a prototype of a pilgrim. She experiences an invitation to realize the Divine within her. The angel assures her that the Divine Power will overshadow her.

Mary's response, "Let it be done to me according to your word," is the perfect response of a pilgrim. Her words could be paraphrased as "Let life happen to me." As a true pilgrim, she flowed with life, being fully present to every "Hosannah!" and every "Crucify him!" moment without clinging to any of them. These were the passing clouds in her life while she kept her anchor in the Eternal Reality.

38. Realizing Bliss

The morning breeze has secrets to tell you.
Do not go back to sleep.

RUMI

We all want to live meaningful and happy lives. Mystics like St. Ignatius of Loyola give us a simple and effective way: pay attention to the last thing at night and the first moments in the morning (Spiritual Exercises, 73–74).

In the first waking moments, we lay out the script for the rest of the day. If our first conscious moments have a positive feel, we will unconsciously find ways to sustain that feeling throughout the day. However, the experience of the first thing in the morning is contingent on the last thing we do at night.

Each night before falling asleep, reflect on the day and recognize, with gratitude, the blessings of the day. Then, as soon as you wake up in the morning, spend the first two minutes of the day in meditation. One way to do this is to sit on your bed and focus on your breathing. See yourself as a flute and your breath as the Divine Essence or Divine Energy passing through every pore of your being, channeling blissful music throughout the rest of the day and every day for the rest of your life.

There is no right way of doing this. Just do it and you will realize the difference! Gratitude is the memory of the heart; the unconscious continues to reveal myriad gifts while we are asleep and is attuned to the gifts that the new day offers. Also, if the first two waking minutes are significant to us, then the unconscious begins the meditation exercise long before we wake up; the Divine Energy or Music flows through our being without our knowing it for the rest of our day until it becomes a way of life.

39. Nothing Exists and Everything Is Alive!

Out beyond ideas of wrongdoing and right doing, there is a field. I'll meet you there. When the soul lies down in that grass, the world is too full to talk about. Ideas, language, even the phrase "each other" does not make any sense.

RUMI

Rumi's invitation is to dwell in the field of the essence of life and experience Bliss, Anand, Shanti, Shalom, Eternal Peace. This field offers freedom from appreciation/criticism, praise/blame, honor/contempt, riches/poverty, pride/humility, success/failure, long life/short life, health/sickness, color/race/gender/sexual orientation. It is to live like the butterfly that is not affected by thorns and roses, or like the lotus flower that is untouched by the dirt all around it.

When the soul finds repose in that field, nothing exists and everything is alive. Perhaps we have had this experience as we sat alone on the beach watching the setting sun and feeling one with the ocean; the day we climbed a slippery roof just to watch the full moon light up the snow-covered mountain range; the time we slept outside in the open countryside and felt one with the canopy of the stars; the day we let ourselves dance in the park as the fall leaves glistened in the golden rays of the setting sun while the mist created a magic land.

Maybe we could find a few moments every day and bring to memory an experience such as that of which Rumi spoke: "When the soul lies down in that grass, the world is too full to talk about. Ideas, language, even the phrase 'each other' does not make sense."

May we live a Bliss-full life!

40. Enlightenment

Knowing others is wisdom, knowing yourself is Enlightenment.

LAO TZU

Enlightenment is one of the innate quests of the human spirit. Everyone, in one form or another, desires enlightenment from the time they are born till the moment of their death. Why, then, does it appear that only a few seem to be enlightened? There are several misconceptions about enlightenment.

Not obtaining or attaining, but a realization

One of these misconceptions is about reaching a goal, particularly if you feel that life is too short and that we need to do all we can to be enlightened. Some try to obtain enlightenment by buying every book or attending every seminar they can find on the topic to better understand it. Others believe they can attain enlightenment if they are part of a group that seeks it through yoga, meditation, and other spiritual practices. All these efforts can keep people scattered and generate frustration and impatience. Often, they will become so emotionally charged about being enlightened that their emotions get in the way of recognizing enlightenment. Enlightenment is neither obtained nor attained. It is an awareness of the reality that just is, at this moment.

We are not chosen; anyone may reach enlightenment

Some are convinced or made to believe that enlightenment is meant for just a chosen few. They look at their lives and are certain that they have never had any experience of that kind. If they notice that at some time or other they had a deeper understanding of life and a sense of profound inner peace and freedom, they think that those experiences were not meant to last. They often compare themselves with the people who proclaim or are acclaimed to be enlightened and are convinced that they do not have the makings of an enlightened person. These, therefore, settle for living a mediocre, mundane life and for never being enlightened.

Enlightenment will not free me from the human condition but free me in the human condition

Many who seek enlightenment believe it will help them attain perfection and experience total freedom from their daily struggles and human problems; no one will dislike them, or at least they will not be affected by others, once they are enlightened. Some people believe they will not have to deal with the challenge of old age or sickness or may even experience a spontaneous cure for any illness they may have. They will have peaked on every level in life: psychological, emotional, and spiritual.

The Buddha faced similar challenges when he was confronted by the reality of sickness, old age, and death. He went through an all-too-familiar path: he first went to the great teachers of his time and outshone them in the knowledge of spiritual realities. He then tried the way of the ascetics and was at the doorstep of death. It was only when he gave up trying to obtain or attain enlightenment that he finally found what he was looking for: true liberation. Just like the *bhikshu* or ascetic he had encountered, he experienced inner freedom and peace amid sickness, old age, death, and all types of human conditions.

Following the pathway of the Buddha, a Zen master made this profound statement: "Before enlightenment, I was depressed. After enlightenment, I am still depressed." The difference is that before the Zen master experienced enlightenment, depression was part of his identity. But after that, he found his essence, and depression was not part of it. He felt like the sky; the depression was like one of those clouds that appeared and moved along without becoming an essential part of the sky.

When you are enlightened, you will know, and the effects will be felt around you. You will not be able to explain or express your experience, but those who have eyes to see will see.

41. Seek the Wizard Within

We carry inside us the wonders we seek outside us.

RUMI

We often look outside ourselves for solutions to our everyday problems and challenges. Like in the great American classic *The Wizard of Oz*, we embark on a search for the Wizard who will provide what is missing in our lives. When we realize that the Wizard cannot really fix us, we discover that all we need is within ourselves.

At the core of our being, we experience peace that the world cannot give and inner bliss that no one and nothing can take away from us. When people see the world falling apart, the peace and bliss within us will transform and transcend this world.

If we get in touch with our essence, we will realize that we are living in the Divine Presence. The music and magic within us will begin to vibrate with the symphony of the Universe. And all will be well!

42. The Birds of the Air and the Lilies of the Field

I want to sing like the birds sing, not worrying about who hears or what they think.

RUMI

Living an authentic life will bring us inner bliss and freedom. When we live by our convictions, it will not matter what others think about us. It does not matter if we are rewarded when we live our passion. Our passion is our reward.

When we follow our passion, we create a divine milieu. In this sacred space, we experience *Wu Wei*, an ancient Chinese principle that means acting without acting. Some translate it as doing nothing. But *Wu Wei* implies being fully immersed in the moment without the dictates of the mind. *Wu Wei*, therefore, is being totally active.

Wu Wei is like water that apparently has no purpose, no goal, and no specific desire, but as it flows, it benefits all of creation without trying to compete with it. It nourishes everything that it passes, without focusing on the results. *Wu Wei* is letting go and going with the flow of the Universe.

As children, we lived in this ecstatic reality, just like the birds and every other part of creation. We had a taste of living in Eternal Bliss and freedom. But we were slowly dragged into the muckiness of life and lost sight of our innocence, freedom, and Divine Essence. However, the deep craving for union with the Divine Source never ceased within us.

The example of the lotus will help us return to a life of freedom and Eternal Bliss. The lotus is rooted in dirt and draws its life and energy from it. Every night it goes back to its roots. But in the morning, it always rises above the chaos and muddy world to manifest itself in all its beauty and charm. It teaches us to celebrate a joy that is always inside us. It is the Eternal Bliss that no one and nothing can take away from us.

43. We Need Inspiration...

I am the master of my fate; I am the captain of my soul.
WILLIAM ERNEST HENLEY

This inspirational quote from the poem "Invictus" by William Ernest Henley expressed Nelson Mandela's foundational life experience. He discovered this poem while he was serving a life sentence on Robben Island, a former leper colony in South Africa. This quote became the meaning and mission of his life; it served as an anchor that kept him grounded when his natural response would have been one of fear, anger, or hatred. Mandela used it as a mantra when he wanted to give up. It inspired him to deal with the difficult times and helped him answer these existential questions: Who am I? What is life all about?

Mandela used his mantra to empower not only those who were in prison with him but also those in charge of that prison. His mantra inspired him to work for reconciliation rather than petty revenge; it helped him to stand alone against the powerful nations of the world.

Mandela believed that we all need inspiration. I have a tremendous sense of intimacy with the Divine Essence. It gives me the courage to jump over the cliffs of life, knowing full well that the Divine Energy will keep me flying beyond sacred boundaries, always seeking new horizons. Being convinced that living with enough is living in abundance helps me enjoy the fullness of life more and more every day. Intimacy with the Divine Essence resonates through every fiber of my being and is expressed by my mantra: *You are Mine!*

44. Unless Your Finger Is Cut Off

If you want to live a happy life, tie it to
a goal not to people or things.
ALBERT EINSTEIN

There is a famous legend of the Zen master who, every time someone asked him the secret of his spiritual life and mysticism, would raise a finger. Every time people would ask one of this master's young disciples what his master's secret was, this young disciple would raise a finger. When the master heard about this disciple, he seized him and cut off his finger. The boy groaned in pain and began to run away. When the Zen master called out to the boy he stopped and turned around. The master raised his finger. At that moment the boy became enlightened and became a Zen master.

This powerful legend makes us reflect on whose lives are we living. Some repeat doctrine, dogmas, and rituals that were handed down to them without ever questioning them. Others follow authors and speakers and quote them without integrating them into their own lives. They have the words but not the music. Like the young disciple in the legend, we all go through a phase of mimicry and imitation. But then we need to be open to the shock of getting our "finger cut off." We must stop, look back, be enlightened, and find our own symbols and expressions of the secret of our own spiritual lives and mysticism.

The finger that is cut off may be security that comes from family, society, culture, religion, and God. The mind, with all the philosophies and theologies, stops; the heart, with all our past experiences, stops; and we are now AWAKE AND ENLIGHTENED. Our lives become models that others follow or envy.

What is the secret of your spiritual life and mysticism, and how will that change the way you live your life? Do you want to be awakened, be enlightened, and allow people to follow you?

45. We Are All Artists

In Art, man reveals himself and not his objects.

RABINDRANATH TAGORE

Just as art is an expression of an inner experience of the artist, so are our personal lives. No true artist will paint the sunset as it is happening; they assimilate the experience in silence and then express it in art. A true dancer becomes one with the dance that flows from their inner spirit. Real prayer comes from the core of our being. We move out of the way and let life happen.

Every action of individuals and groups is an expression of who we truly are. Our relationships with God, family, and others are also a reflection of who we are. Often, we see the world and life not as *it* is but as *we* are.

True life, like art, is a spontaneous expression of our essence and blends with the Divine Essence that is present in every part of creation.

46. Ablaze without Being Consumed

If light is in your heart, you will find your way home.
Set your life on fire. Seek those who fan your flames.
Dance until you shatter yourself.

RUMI

The Buddha's very last teaching was to be lamps unto ourselves. We need to live from the core of our being. It is at this core where the Divine resides as spiritual energy or sacred fire. It is here where we will find our essence intrinsically comingled with the Divine Essence.

We need people who can meet us at our core and keep the fire at our core glowing. These people are not only the ones who share our passion for life but also those who think and live life very differently from us.

The fire within also has the power to burn all negative and false beliefs. It will purify us of all our negative and painful experiences without leaving a scar. The more we take care of the flame within us, the more the world around us will come alive. Like the burning bush that Moses witnessed, we can be on fire without being consumed. In the glow of this fire, our lives will burst forth into a spontaneous dance.

47. Fly and Find Your Authentic Self

You were born with wings;
why prefer to crawl through life?
RUMI

When we realize the gifts that we are born with, we begin to find our wings and experience exhilarating energy; we find a new perspective on life. When we crawl through life, we cannot see the stars or experience the beauty and magic all around us. But when we fly through life, everything looks expansive and feels different.

Sometimes we do not realize our true potential until we let go of our long-held securities. We need to break through the walls of culture and tradition. It is said that when God pushes you to the edge, only two things can happen: either He will catch you when you fall, or He will teach you how to fly. The question is: Do you jump off the cliff and expect God and people to catch you, thereby becoming codependent, or are you ready to fly in freedom?

When we begin to fly, we move beyond sacred boundaries seeking new horizons. We will find people who will be the wind beneath our wings, encouraging us to trace our unique and authentic path in life. We leave our mark in life to help others find their own wings and fly.

48. Conventions and Change Come with a Price

Conventional opinion is the ruin of our souls.

RUMI

Society develops conventional systems for its proper functioning. These structures are rooted in tradition, culture, religion, and social values. However, all these arrangements are also timebound; slowly but surely, this conventional wisdom will have all convention and little wisdom. How often conventional wisdom rooted in the past without any critical thinking has caused division, hatred, and even the death of individuals and groups.

If everyone thinks that something is right, there might be something wrong. Just because something was good and right in the past does not mean it will be the same today and forever. We need to look at reality and conventional truth with new eyes. With greater clarity and critical thinking, we will find new and creative ways of understanding reality and living meaningful lives.

Life is always fluid. Change and transformation are the very nature of life. For our soul to be alive, it needs to be in the flow of life. Structures that block this flow will stagnate the soul and life itself.

Heraclitus of Ephesus (c. 500 BCE) claimed that life is in a constant state of flux. This is often explained as "you cannot step into the same river twice." Every time you step into the river, you and the river have changed. His contemporary, Siddhartha Gautama, the Buddha (c. 563–483 BCE), also recognized that nothing was permanent; everything was in a constant state of change. The cause of suffering was people's insistence on permanence in a world of impermanence.

Openness alone is not enough for change. Openness is not the end; it is only the beginning. Change comes at a price. A prophet usually ends up being killed. Sometimes people who fight for change are alienated, punished, and made to suffer by the people they love the most.

Because of this consequence of change, many people choose to remain silent. This silence is more damaging than facing the conflict of change. In the words of Martin Luther King Jr., "In the end, we will remember not the words of our enemies, but the silence of our friends."

49. Welcome the Dawn

Death is not extinguishing the light; it is only putting
out the lamp because the dawn has come.

RABINDRANATH TAGORE

Shakespeare believed that "The valiant never taste of death but once" (*Julius Caesar*, II, ii, 32–37), but in fact, we die many times while we are still alive to prepare for our final passing. The innocence of the child has to die for them to welcome the dawn of adventurous youth. Yet, if we hold on to our youth and adult life, we cannot experience the wisdom and freedom of old age.

We die to the myths and fairy tales of childhood and accept the dawn of philosophies and doctrines. But are we willing to risk dying to all that sustains us at the adult stage so we can welcome the wisdom of the sages? We thus return once again to the mystical and magical life of the child. The Kingdom of God belongs to little children.

We also know that "unless a grain of wheat falls into the earth and dies, it remains just a single grain; but if it dies, it bears much fruit" (John 12:24). The question is this: How far are we willing to go down the rabbit hole to get rid of material, mental, emotional, and spiritual clutter so our lives will bear abundant fruit? We must abandon our selfish, insecure selves that want to control and direct life and let our authentic selves come alive and flow with life with the confidence and ease of the birds of the air and the lilies of the field.

If we have the courage to extinguish the light of our present way of relating with God and everything that sustains it, we will experience the dawn of an exhilarating relationship with the Infinite Logos, "Energy charged with Power," the Divine Breath, *THAT*!

50. When You Know How to Die

If I know I will die tomorrow,
I can still learn something tonight.

TIBETAN PROVERB

When you know how to die, you will know how to live. Once we recognize the transitoriness of life, we look for the source of our happiness and the meaning of our lives. When we find that this source is what gives life and energy to all of creation, we will realize that we are an integral part of the flow of this Eternal Energy. When we begin to live every moment as fully as we can, all of life becomes a celebration. Our inner bliss breaks out into a glorious dance.

Realizing that all of life is transitory, we celebrate the paradox of impermanence. This reality brings us face to face with our own mortality. On one hand, it frightens us; on the other hand, it spurs us on to live where we fear to live, physically, emotionally, and spiritually. We find the courage to be different and to live our most authentic and fulfilling life. We look at all our relationships, possessions, and positions in life and know for the first time that we came into this world alone and with nothing, and we will leave the same way. We let go of all our fears and begin to live our most authentic lives. We look forward to dying while living our purpose and passion.

51. Birth of a Dancing Star

You need chaos in your soul to give birth to a dancing star.

FRIEDRICH NIETZSCHE

At the beginning of every new year, there is an urgency around breaking forth into a new realm of life and reality. It sometimes feels scary, sometimes even out of control, but there seems to be no stopping it. Something within is proclaiming: The world as we know it is gone, the life we have lived is over, and the God we thought we knew does not exist anymore. We experience chaos and darkness, all around us and in different parts of the world, but we remember that from chaos and darkness we have the first account of creation in the Bible. This chaos is birthing a dancing star.

We are living at an exciting time, where the past is fading away and life is opening to a new reality. The barriers that were created to divide the world are crumbling and bringing us closer as one human family. The materialistic life that we strive for is now offering us the spiritual and mystical. The God that we grew up with has burst into stardust, giving us the profound experiences and sensitivities of the Divine, beyond words and human understanding. It is a challenge to let go of our human existence and give birth to our divine essence.

We are moving from the baptism of Water, to the baptism of Fire, through the baptism of the Spirit. We are growing from a religious people to a spiritual group and are now part of a mystical entity. Religious people are initiated by the baptism of Water—water that symbolizes purification and life. In Carl Jung's psychology, water is the symbol of the collective unconsciousness.

When we are baptized in water, we accept the faith and tradition of a group of people. We need doctrine, dogmas, rituals, and membership in a community to sustain us. When we experience the baptism of the Spirit, our relationship with God becomes personal; doctrines, dogmas, and rituals are no longer absolutes but means to help us deepen this relationship. Our relationship with God overflows to all peoples; we open ourselves to people of all faiths and cultural traditions. Baptism of Fire purifies and frees us from dogma, doctrine, and ritual. This stage is a process of continually emptying the self and all that sustains it. It is an invitation to give up our human identity, live in the Divine Essence, and experience oneness with all of creation, where no hierarchy exists. We become the drop in the ocean and experience the ocean in the drop. In fact, we become the ocean!

52. When the Student Is Ready

When the student is ready the teacher will appear.
When the student is truly ready...the teacher will disappear.
LAO TZU

When we look at nature, we find that every creature nurtures its young until they are ready to leave the nest and live independent lives. Parent birds begin to teach their fledglings to fly by staying a short distance from the nest during feeding. The fledgling must then step outside of the nest to receive the food. This results in many hard falls, during which the young bird begins to learn the mechanics of flight.

Eventually, the parent bird no longer needs to be present to the fledgling. Flight becomes instinctive, and the young bird goes off to start a family of its own.

We see a parallel pattern with land animals. The little ones are taught to fend for themselves and defend themselves against any adversary. They learn by watching and imitating their parents. Timing is everything. If the lessons stop too early, it will mean the death of the young ones. However, in time, the youth no longer needs the parent's example. It has learned what is necessary for defense and survival.

Now let us turn to Mary Magdalene, who longed to leave behind a life void of love or joy. As she listened to this new teacher from Galilee, her heart began to stir. Jesus spoke of the love of God. From him, she realized her Divine Identity. She followed Jesus and listened carefully to his teachings. She became one of his most loyal disciples, drinking in every word and taking to heart every act of compassion.

All seemed lost when he was put to death, but she remained loyal. This loyalty and desire to follow Jesus' teachings were affirmed when, after the Resurrection, Jesus appeared to her first. But as she reached to embrace him, he taught her one last lesson: "Do not cling to me" (John 20:17). *She no longer needed to cling to his every word and action; she was ready to continue his ministry in her own way.* Jesus, her *Rabboni* (teacher), "disappeared."

May this be true of you and me. Yes, we are drawn to sages and gurus for their deep insights into the existential questions of life.

In God's grace, we willingly apprentice ourselves to Jesus, the master teacher. And as we soak up the depth of his teaching, his way of life, we eventually find ourselves not clinging—but nudged from the nest, liberated to experience bliss ever onward.

In every age and generation, certain individuals have deep insights into the existential questions. In ancient times, seekers of the truth would join a community of priest-sages who treasured this secret wisdom. These seekers were sincere followers of their religion who were left either unfulfilled or just wanting more. Having explored the well of their formal religion, they encountered the source of that well, namely, the ocean of God's love and life. They needed guidance and help to move beyond the well. They believed that the community of priest-sages would give them that wisdom.

As a novice, each of them would have a prolonged period of preparation and testing. When the sages found one who was ready, they would lead that individual stage by stage away from the earthly life and transport them to some hidden world in the mystical realm. Step by step all the senses would be brought under the control of the Spirit, and the novice would begin to experience the secret wisdom of the ancient sages and to live more and more like a spiritual being.

Sometimes a stage is reached when the seeker dies to the old self but no new self emerges. All of life seems to be death! This could be the end of the road for some—but if they persevere then this death brings about a transfiguration, a new way of living life. This human life continues to die many deaths before a person experiences life in all its fullness. The novice is now no longer dependent on the priest-sages but becomes a master, leading others along the path of freedom and enlightenment.